Nine Seasons:
Beyond 2012

A Manual

Of Ancient Aztec & Maya Wisdom

By Carlos Aceves (Yolohuitzcalotl)

This book is published, released, and distributed by:
Indigenous Cultures Institute
P.O. Box 1414, San Marcos, Texas 78667,
www.IndigenousCultures.org

Written by **Carlos Aceves**, M.Ed.
© 2012 by Carlos Aceves, M.Ed.

Cover design and illustrations by **Gabriel S. Gaytán**, Gaytán Artworks,
El Paso, Texas, www.gaytanartworks.com

Edited by **Tammy Gonzales**

ISBN-10: 0615615228
ISBN-13: 978-0-615-61522-6

INDIGENOUS CULTURES
INSTITUTE

Indigenous Cultures Institute is a nonprofit organization that promotes and preserves the cultures of Native Americans indigenous to Texas and northern Mexico, and maintains our covenant with sacred sites. The Institute focuses on the indigenous heritage of Hispanics whose ancestors are primarily Coahuiltecan people from the Rio Grande Delta.

For more information, visit www.IndigenousCultures.org.

TABLE OF CONTENTS

A Mesoamerican metaphoric counting system blending numbers with natural phenomenon to express ancient knowledge.

The number thirteen provides a numerical pattern used to synchronize human cycles with those of Mother Nature.

Celestial cycles can be used to meditate and help us be in harmony with Creation.

There are seven skills a human being needs to learn and practice to be able to live 104 years.

The Mesoamerican diet is organized around seven basic foods that provide enhanced nutrition.

Human gestation is marked by five crucial events that can be augmented by parental and community participation.

Humans are designed to have a life span of 104 years which can be divided into nine stages.

Visualizing death as a journey with nine challenges teaching us to have a good death, which is important to living a good life.

An explanation of our responsibilities as part of the seven generations of Life.

Nahuatl and Spanish terms used in the text.

Author's Comments

As you read this manual, you may ask from where does this information come? Who were the ancient ones? The simple answer is that they were people from a time long ago who made it their life's mission to learn and teach a natural way of life. This work uses the knowledge of the Aztecs and Mayans. Ancients such as these existed all over the world and for many centuries. Every culture today can find them in the family tree of its own history. But we need not go back in time to find the ancients. Look in the mirror and then inside your heart. Can you visualize the children of your grandchildren and find the desire to offer them an Earth that will provide for them in the same way as all mothers provide for their children? If the answer is yes, then you may be an ancient.

You will notice that this book is written as a "we" rather than an "I." The manual is a work that has many authors. Life has blessed me with good, loving teachers who can also be called ancients. The work behind this manual was also a collaborative effort. Therefore, the narrative speaks in the "We."

We have also capitalized many words that otherwise would not require capitalization. This is to honor the many forces of nature such as Sun, Moon, Earth, and Seasons. They too are alive. They influence and give us Life. Now we understand why fathers and mothers would always cut their hair on a full or waning Moon. Being less susceptible to the fertility created by a waxing Moon, the hair would grow slower, extending the time between haircuts.

Finally, this written work is dedicated to three personal heroes: Elpidia Vargas Lopez, my mother who suffered much giving birth to me and later endured years of physical pain until

1

her death but created in me a deep faith for the paths of nature; Paola Lopez Juarez, who treated me more like her own son than her student and, though she could heal with her hands, still knew all the medicinal herbs and their applications; and Isabel Quevedo Plascencia, who carried out enormous work for the revival of the ancient art of making and marketing honey from the maguey (agave) plant, a product now used world-wide. Through these three women, I experienced and learned about that powerful force of the Universe which makes anything possible: Love.

Introduction

My wife and I have known Carlos for a very long time. I even adopted him as a brother in a peyote ceremony almost twenty years ago. I have always been impressed by his knowledge and understanding of different ancient philosophies, especially the Aztec and Mayan wisdom. I look forward to his visits as we always stay up late discussing ancient beliefs. We, at Indigenous Cultures Institute, continually invite him to our area to share his knowledge. He has conducted activities for children, workshops for our Indigenous community, and lectures in our San Marcos community and in nearby Austin, Texas.

Unfailingly, I learn something from all of my interactions with Carlos. Sometimes I have been inclined to write down his teachings, but mostly I hope to remember all the things he says, at least the most important ones. So I was very pleased to receive the draft of his manuscript for *Nine Seasons* because it contained much of the information that he had previously given us, and this time it was in writing. Now I have a quick reference to any details that I might have forgotten.

This manual is full of information and knowledge presented in a very simple way. It is truly a great gift that allows us to grasp some of the wisdom that our ancestors acquired a long time ago. It starts with a *cuenta* or metaphorical count in which numbers are assigned to natural phenomenon as a very simple means of storing knowledge. It is an indigenous method of combining several disciplines in one activity in order to teach. I have seen Carlos' students numerous times recite this *cuenta* and wish that I had been taught this as a child.

Carlos goes on to discuss the power of the number thirteen and how thirteen relates to the cosmos but also to our own bodies. In the third chapter, he discusses sky meditations and how we can get significant blessings just by observing a sunrise. Chapter Four is about seven activities that we are born knowing but soon forget. We need to relearn these and practice them for good health.

Chapter Five is an amazing description of the important indigenous foods that we call the seven warrior foods which we need for good health. Chapter Six is about our journey through the womb and how it consists of five special events and the four spaces of time in between. Chapter Seven is about our nine seasons from the beginning of life in the womb through the last 91 to 104 years of life. This chapter teaches us how to be responsible for ourselves while carrying out our tasks and maintaining our authenticity. Chapter Eight is about our death. It describes the three processes of death and the nine challenges of a good death.

The last chapter, Chapter Nine, has been completely changed from the first edition. Chapter Nine explains the concept of the "Seventh Generation" and how, if we are to save and protect Mother Earth, we need to consider that every action that changes our Earth must be weighed against how it will affect our seventh generation.

I feel very honored to write this introduction. This manual provides a very simple and easy way to comprehend and incorporate some ancient Aztec and Mayan teachings into our everyday lives. In following these concepts, we can learn how to live a happy 104-year-old life.

Happy Reading,
Mario Garza, Ph.D. (Tza Yan Tamōx)
Indigenous Cultures Institute

CHAPTER ONE: Cuentos y Cuentas

"Long ago people practiced the Tao. They maintained balance of body and mind. It is not surprising that they were able to live over one hundred years."
The Neijin Suwen
(The Yellow Emperor's Guide to Internal Medicine)
China, 240 B.C.

This is a wonderful time to be alive and aware! Our ancestors throughout the world spoke of this age over 5,000 years ago. For some, this means the planets are aligning as they have not done before. For others it is a shift in consciousness. Some may see it as the end of time, while others choose to interpret it as a new beginning. This is a moment of celebration primarily because we are aware of the infinite possibilities. What is certain is that the prophecy of the ancients pointed to this time.

We celebrate because we have an opportunity to change the vibration of human existence and redirect our connection with Mother Earth. Look within. Contemplate your relationship to community, nature, and the Great Spirit. Being grateful is the beginning of celebration. The awareness of where we are brings us to the most important window of time, which is Now.

Many of the lessons in this manual are from Mesoamerica. However, they are universal in scope and spirit. Before religions, our ancestors were spiritual because they respected nature. In nature, they found the lessons that taught them a healthy path of living. The basic duties and functions of humankind, such as breathing, drinking, eating, sleeping, or procreating, are integral to our relationship with Mother Creation. We can look back at cultures that practiced a natural way of life and use that knowledge to create for ourselves a world that offers Health, Happiness, and Love.

A human life can span 104 years over a period of nine seasons or stages. Our trust in this statement comes from ancient traditions. This manual can make a 104-year life a reality. A lifetime does not have to become an endeavor anguished by aging but a journey enhanced by the Spirit of Life. Creation has placed before us the means to carry out such an adventure. We invite you to become travelers on this path.

Allow us to begin this mystical trek with a *cuento*, a story, from the ancients that illustrates we need not look too far to find Truth. It is said that when humans were once again placed upon Mother Earth after the great flood, the Creators were unsure where to place the secret of Life so that humans could not find it. Such knowledge could not be entrusted to creatures as unreliable as humans. Several animals suggested where to put it.

Eagle said, "I will take it to the highest mountain where no human could ever climb." But everyone knew that eventually people would discover a way to fly and find the secret.

Turtle suggested, "Let me take it to the bottom of the sea. Humans cannot hold their breath long enough to get there." But everyone knew humans would surely invent a way to breathe underwater.

Then Deer had the best idea of all. "Place it in their hearts. They will never think of looking there." So it was done, and, in truth, few of us ever seek our heart to find answers.

What resides inside this continually beating, blood-pumping organ is not just knowledge but a key that opens the door to our own understanding. Indeed, a Toltec proverb says that "the path to wisdom lies in dialogue with your own heart." What is it that we are to understand? Simply, how to live as Mother Creation demonstrates.

This information and knowledge was gathered for us long ago. Another ancient *cuento* relates how millennia ago two children were born whose destiny was to be incarnations of two powerful spirits of Creation—Earth Woman *Tlalcihuatl* and Sky Chief *Tlaltecutli*. Their own names were different, *Cipactonal* and *Oxomoco (fig. 1)*. This happened so long ago that people are no longer sure which gender goes with which name. That is not as important as their mission: to dedicate their lifetimes to observing and recording the movements of Earth and Sky.

Fig. 1 Parents of Humanity

Oxomoco and Cipactonal

With their study lasting well over a century, they gathered enough information to create synchronized wheels of knowledge. This wisdom was, and continues to be, handed across generations so that we know how to live as members of the family of Creation. Through this kinship, we are offered a lifespan of 104 years. Today, these synchronized wheels, called *Tonal Machiotl* and *Tonalpohualli*, are part of the Aztec and Mayan Calendars, astronomical instruments full of information and knowledge that once served two cultures of Middle America. Today, it can be beneficial for the whole of humanity.

Information when codified becomes knowledge. When knowledge is applied, it becomes wisdom. Although this is not an intense course in astronomy, nor do we pretend to know all that *Cipactonal* and *Oxomoco* learned in decades of scientific observation, it is useful to understand some basic astronomical premises for what they called *Tonalpohualli,* the solar count. Included are also some philosophical principles, not so much a jewel for the mind to ponder but a tool to make it easier for the heart to embrace.

What these ancestors created is as universal as it is simple. It is gifted to us in a form that allows us to be able to grasp the knowledge that they discovered. To those that wish to pursue this path, we encourage you. There are plenty of traditional teachers and sources that will make this task possible. We present what can more appropriately be called a manual, easily understood and simple to apply; but, we give notice from the start that discipline is required.

The Aztec-Mayan Calendar is only one of several ways this information is kept. Another is what is called a "metaphorical count" in which numbers are assigned to natural phenomenon as a mnemonic means of storing knowledge. There are several versions of this *cuenta,* or count, such as those found in the works of Domingo Martínez Paredes and Hunbatz Men, both traditional Mayan teachers. Others are found in oral tradition such as when someone is told "you are a twenty" (to mean one is complete) or "when you have nothing you have everything." This *cuenta* is also the source of the title for our manual, *Nine Seasons*, referring to the nine seasons of Life. This count of time has very ancient Mesoamerican roots.

Here is the *cuenta* followed by an explanation:

Zero is Infinity. Zero is nothing and nothing is infinite. Before becoming One, we were Zero. We become One by coming from Infinity. Zero is a spiral, forever unfolding and forever folding inward. When the spiral closes it forms a circle; thus, Zero becomes One. But a circle retains its inward spiral and so our center is our gateway to infinity.

One is the Sun. We have only one Sun, our one source of heat. We have one universal father whose union with Earth creates each form of life including humans.

Two is the Earth. Earth is an embodiment of opposites: up-down, night-day, female-male, liquid-solid, and hot-cold; Earth's innate duality creates Life.

Three are the Animals. There are animals of the land, sky, and water. They teach us how to relate to the three parts of our environment: earth, sky (air), and water. They also tell us about our "animal stages"—in the womb we swim and breathe like fish; when we are born, we crawl upon the earth; and as we grow, consciousness allows us to "leap" and "fly" like birds.

Four are the People. We procreate through the pattern of four: mother, father, daughter, and son. We have four main extensions (limbs) and we embody the four elements (fig. 2): fire, earth, water, and air.

Fig. 2 The Four Limbs

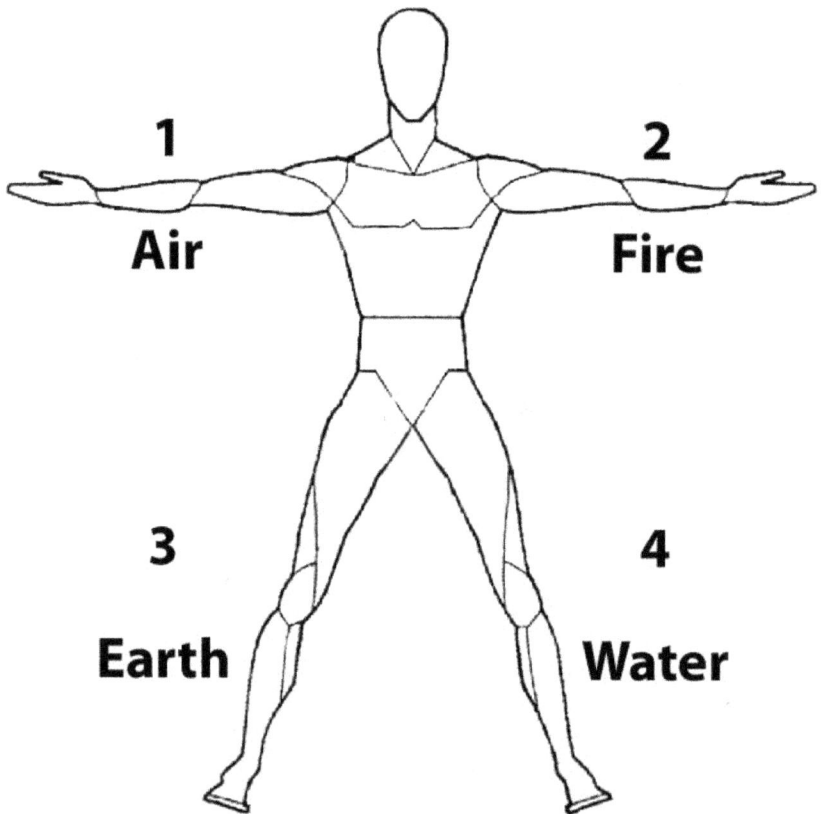

Five is the World. With the work of the five fingers of each hand we transform Earth into a World as when we change a tree into a table.

Six is the Sky. There are six things of the sky which allow us to measure existence (time): Sun, Moon, stars, clouds, Morning Star, and Evening Star.

Seven is the Moon. The Moon has seven faces. (fig. 3)

Fig. 3

Seven Faces of the Moon

Eight are the Birds. When we open our hands, they look like birds. Our right hand represents Venus as Morning Star and our left hand Venus as Evening Star (fig. 4). They come together and form one bird with two heads. This is a mnemonic gesture representing the five patterns of Venus (five fingers) that repeat every eight years (fingers forming the bird's wings). It also means that Evening Star and Morning Star are one.

Fig. 4 Venus

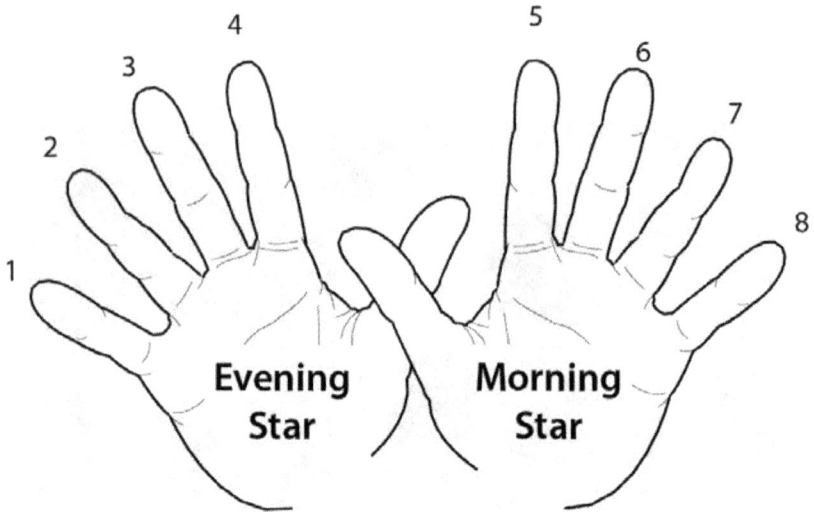

Nine are the Seasons. There are nine seasons in a human life over a span of 104 years. Every thirteen years we undergo a transformation of body, mind, and soul. Here are a few ways to view this process.

In one lifetime, a human has the capacity to achieve seven transformations after birth. This puts a person at age 91. It is then possible to live at least another thirteen years. Our time in the womb is the first season. Each transformation is also a season (seven). Our last thirteen years before death is our ninth season.

Another way to view this process is to divide a human life into two parts, each 52 years. The first half is our receiving or *Teacatlipoca* years and the second is our giving or *Quetzalcoatl* years. Each part in turn has four stages, giving us a total of eight plus our season in the womb makes nine.

Ten is Death. After season nine, we die.

Eleven are the Waters. After death, life returns through water. We are made inside a bag of water and we breathe like fish.

Twelve is Community. We are born into a community. Our body is a community of twelve main joints that allows us to move. (fig. 5)

Fig. 5 The Community

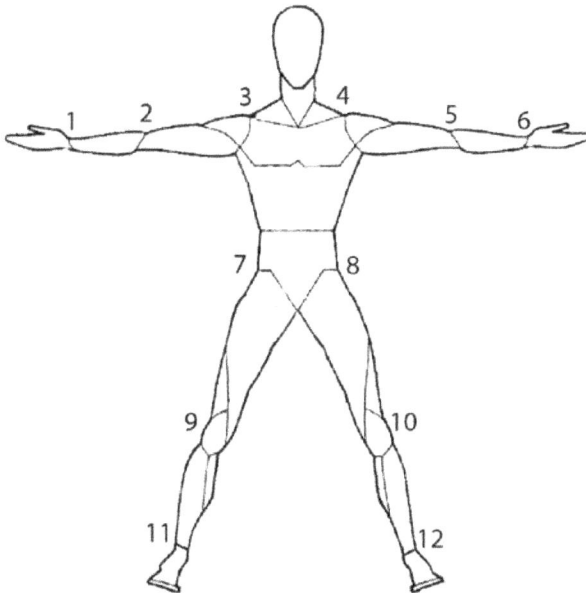

Twelve main joints work together as a community allowing us movement

Thirteen are the Stars. Our "thirteenth joint" is our neck, which allows us to tilt the head and see the sky. The stars represent thoughts. Their patterns represent knowledge. Through our thirteen moveable parts, we are able to apply this knowledge. In other versions of the "metaphorical count," the number thirteen is wisdom.

Numbers fourteen through nineteen are considered composites of the previous numbers.

Twenty is Complete. When we have the twenty digits of our hands and fingers we are complete. It takes 260 days inside the womb for a human body to become complete (13 x 20 = 260). But, we need thirteen more days for our electromagnetic centers (chakras) to connect and then we are born (260 + 13 = 273).

We are confident that this *cuenta* will be useful to you in reading, understanding, and applying the concepts of this manual.   We will provide references to some of this information. The count contains the knowledge gathered by *Cipactonal* and *Oxomoco*, though it is not our purpose to explore every aspect of it. Again, we turn the focus to our own heart and, as we learn this natural form of counting, it is from there that answers will arise.

CHAPTER TWO: The Power of Thirteen

"The thirteenth level of Creation is the essence of total inactivity,
complete silence from which all existence blossoms
between duality and death."
Carmen Nieva, Mexikayotl

In one of the early Star Trek television shows, a species from another part of the galaxy upon encountering humans began referring to them as "ugly bags of mostly water." Although humorous, this is an accurate description of what we are. Earth herself is a vessel of mostly water and this composition makes it possible for her to use the Sun's heat to create weather, seasons, geological changes, and an abundance of life forms. We also know that Earth's water is pulled by the Moon's gravity creating not only ocean tides but an ebb and flow in the fluids of all Earth bodies. That is why a tree is cut for furniture making when the Moon is new and the wood is not yet full of liquid. Those that know, plant according to Moon cycles because each seed reacts differently to the percentage of the soil's moisture. The ancients were very much aware that as "bags of mostly water" humans are also influenced by the Sun and Moon.

Do we not rotate as Earth rotates? Do we not move around the Sun as the Earth orbits? Does not the Moon orbit us as she moves around Earth? As bodies of water we also have something akin to internal weather patterns, seasons, physical changes, and continual life and death cycles as our bodies grow and renew. We need to be aware of how our position and movement as smaller celestial bodies react to our relatives in the sky and Mother Earth. By gaining this awareness, we can use our own celestial motion across the universe to maintain the cosmic flow which makes for a long and healthy life.

Our metaphorical count relates how the number thirteen, which represents knowledge, can be formed by adding twelve main joints of our body to the ability to move our heads. Another way of relating thirteen to human beings is to realize that a woman's menstruation cycle is in synchronicity with the Moon. Just as there are thirteen full Moons in a year, a woman is also fertile thirteen times a year. This number also comes up when we examine the seven portholes through which we perceive or "take in" the world and the six directions of their focus: two ears, two eyes, two nostrils, and one mouth makes seven (fig. 6). They perceive the world in front, back, left side, right side, up, and down (six). Seven plus six equals thirteen.

Fig. 6 Seven Portholes of Perception

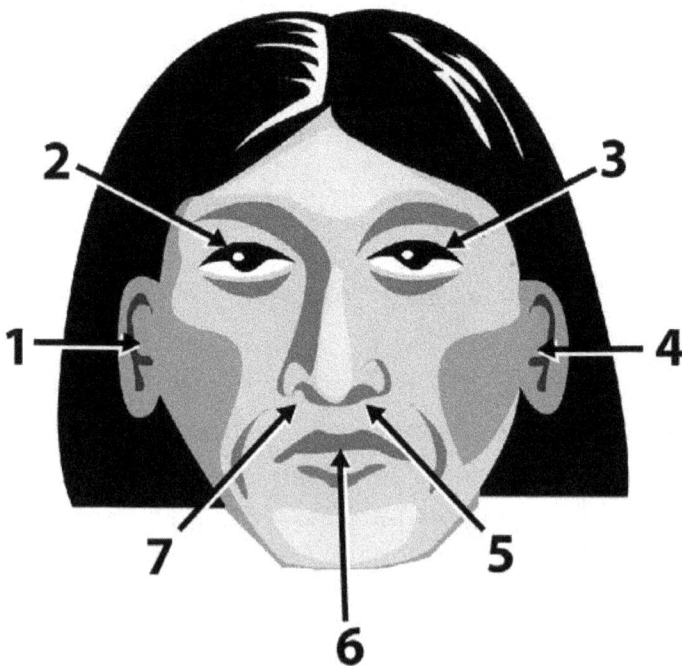

Another way the number thirteen comes up is by adding the number of portholes and their functions. The ear's function is to listen and, as an internal gyroscope, to balance our bodies so we do not tip over as we stand or walk. The eyes are to see by dividing visual information into two parts, going to the left and right brain. The ancients called this "sight of reason and sight of knowing." The nostrils are for breathing and smelling. Our mouths perceive the world by tasting. Thus, seven portholes plus six functions is thirteen.

There are many ways to organize the number of body parts into patterns. As we reference our *cuenta,* we will see other examples and have a better understanding of why the ancients did this. Humans are products of the union of a female and male, growing from a microscopic size into a form able to function outside the womb. This is our first season and there is a correlation between this process and the astronomy of Earth, Sun, and Moon. First, let us realize that our conception is a lunar occurrence since women's fertility cycles are tied to the Moon. A Moon cycle can be divided into three parts: waning, waxing, and the transition time between both. What the ancients discovered is that the waning and waxing power of the Moon can be divided into thirteen days of waxing force and thirteen days of waning force. The transition time accounts for a Moon cycle adding up to roughly 29 days.

Just as the Moon orbits us as she does Earth, we also orbit the Sun as our home planet moves around him. By examining Earth's journey around the Sun, we again find the number thirteen in a significant way. Simple astronomy tells us that in a period of one Earth orbit or year, our planet also experiences four key transitions: winter, spring, fall, and summer. The ancients also knew that there are four other important positions of Earth in relation to the Sun:

- Thirteen days after Summer Solstice, she is at her farthest position from the Sun.

- Thirteen days after Winter Solstice, she is at her closest position to the Sun.

- Thirteen days after Fall Equinox, she is at the same distance from the Sun as she is at thirteen days after Spring Equinox.

- Thirteen days after the Spring Equinox, she is the same distance from the Sun as she is thirteen days after the Fall Equinox.

Astronomers today call these positions perihelion (closest), aphelion (farthest), and equihelion (equidistant). These positions are an integral part of the Aztec Calendar with deeper implications.

Tracking Earth from her perihelion point to her position at the spring equinox we discover a total of 260 days. Thirteen days later, she is at an equihelion point, which adds up to 273. The ancients discovered that Earth's orbit can be divided into patterns of 260 and 273, in which thirteen plays a part. We know that between summer solstice and spring equinox there are 273 days. The same is true between spring equinox and winter solstice, between winter solstice and fall equinox, and between fall equinox and summer solstice. Likewise, there are 260 days between the fall equihelion and summer solstice,

18

between perihelion and fall equinox, between spring equihelion and winter solstice, and between aphelion and spring equinox.

These numbers are important to the human gestation cycle. We know that it takes 273 days to form a human being inside the womb. We also know that at 260 days a human body is complete, but the ancients tell us that thirteen more days are needed for our animation forces, our electromagnetic centers, to begin connecting with each other as part of an integration process that will last an entire lifetime. Thus, the same numbers are at play in Earth's orbit as there are in the human gestation cycle: 260, 273, and thirteen. This 260 cycle is called *tonalpohualli*, the wheel in the Aztec Calendar that reflects in the integration of human cycles with those of the Earth, Moon, and Sun.

Our four animating forces are products of the spiritual force that created us and the four elements that form us. Our *tonalli* first appears above our fontanel, the hollow crevice atop our infant heads. *Tonalli* literally means "solar vibration" or our solar fire. *Teyolia* appears at our heart's center enveloping the pericardium. It is our heart-spirit. Below our liver is our *ihiyotl,* a greenish gas created from earth and fire that generates our passions. Within our bladder is the *atlachinolli*, the fire that moves like water and forms meridians throughout our bodies, equivalent to the Chinese *chi*. Integration of these four, and their properly working together, is vital for maintaining our health.

Each journey through our mother's body is also divided into nine stages consisting of five pivotal moments and the time in between. The first moment is our nesting or attaching to the womb and forming the structure that will sustain our growth.

Formation of a "nest" takes thirteen days after a woman becomes pregnant. Second is the completion of our heart at 52 days. Third is the construction of our brain and nervous systems at 169 days. Fourth is the nestling of our *tonalli* on our fontanel at 260 days. Finally, there is the "breaking of the fountain" at 273 days when the liquid that sustained us is released. Our birthing, of course, follows this. Notice the role of thirteen across these stages. Nesting takes thirteen days. Fifty-two is a product of 4 x 13. One hundred sixty-nine is 13 x 13. Two hundred sixty is 13 x 20. Water is released thirteen days after the appearance of the *tonalli*.

Those who constructed the Aztec-Mayan Calendar made the number thirteen the key to their count. There are twenty days in the day-wheel (fig. 7) that are counted one through thirteen. After thirteen, the count returns to one. They also divided the night sky into thirteen constellations so that their movement across a year's time tells the story of Creation. One of those constellations, Cygnus, they called the "Tree of Life" which gets "watered" as the meteorite shower on August 13 appears from our vantage point to fall over this constellation. August 13, 3117 B.C. was chosen as the birth date of this era, the Age of Corn, which will last until August 13, 2012, and is part of the Calendar returning to a zero point on December 21, 2012.

Our bodies also undergo important changes that can be tracked using thirteen. As we explained in "Nine are the seasons," a human body undergoes important changes every thirteen years. Thus, key ages to note are 13, 26, 39, 52, 65, 78, 91, and 104. More will be explained about how to use these age numbers. Another tracking method is counting by days. A body functions in cycles of thirteen days and we need to not only be aware of it but use it to organize our daily living so we keep ourselves in rhythm with Creation. Our next chapter will focus on how to do this.

CHAPTER THREE: Sky Meditations

*"Our Anahuac civilization was not plagued by conflicts over religion for
our culture is scientific."*
Arturo Meza, Tonalpohuaki

The Sun

Every day the Sun offers us a gift; we simply have to show up to get it. To those following a natural way of life, oversleeping simply means getting up after the Sun has already risen. It is important to greet the Sun as he is rising for in those first rays of sunlight are a blessing for the day. Many call the Sun father or grandfather. They consider waiting for him to come over the horizon a way of showing respect for an elder. This honoring is one of the blessings you receive as twilight breaks. Those first rays of our grandfather trigger endorphins in the brain which give an emotional boost for the day, something which has been proven by modern science.. One of the side effects of this boost is a strengthening of our immune system. These are significant blessings just for standing and waiting for the Sun to rise. Of course if we begin our day with this practice, then honoring the sunset is also a good way of setting closure for our day.

Evening and Morning Stars

If you greet the sky on a regular basis, there are two objects that will surely get your attention: Venus (as Morning and Evening Star) and the Moon. Venus is the last "star" to remain as the sunlight overwhelms the eastern horizon. Among other things, she is a symbol of the pericardium. The pericardium is the electrode at the center of the heart which makes this organ contract to pump blood. The Sun represents the heart because, as he travels across the sky, he leans to the south in the same way our hearts lean to the left. This leaning motion is called *Huitzilopochtli* (left-leaning or southern-leaning hummingbird). A recommended morning meditation is to use the Morning Star and Sun as a way to visualize a good heartbeat for that day.

Venus as the Evening Star also has a message. Sometime after sunset she will go out of view. This disappearance symbolizes falling asleep and entering into our dream state. Metaphorically, it was said that the Evening Star became a dog spirit named *Xolotl* who went to the underworld with the ability to rescue lost souls. We can use the Evening Star to visualize our own entrance into our dreams and ask *Xolotl* to help find us peace with whatever psychological trouble we are taking to our sleep. We need not analyze what troubles us, but simply give it to the servant spirit of night, that wise part of ourselves that works best when we are unconscious. It is said the *Xolotl's* power comes from his ability to become any form in the netherworld participating in whatever drama comes up and then instantly returning to his authentic self. He is flexible, playful, detached yet deeply caring.

The Moon

While we are watching the evening or early morning sky, it is also useful to observe the Moon and take note of what face she is allowing us to see that day. Think of her face as a reminder of where our introspective focus might be at the time. An empty face (new Moon) and a full Moon are transition times. When the Moon reaches her full position, her force has drawn towards her thirteen days of the fluids of all living beings. As she empties, she is releasing her hold on them. When the Moon is waxing, Earth's fertility is rising—a prime time for planting depending on the waxing phase. Each seed has its own corresponding time to each phase. For example, the best time to plant squash is during a waxing crescent. Within us all our fluids, including our blood, are being pulled and energized by the Moon. It is a good time to move a little faster with tasks or push a bit harder. As she enters waning, the Moon is releasing and it may be a good time to slow down or not push so hard. The best time to cut a tree to be used for furniture is between the waning crescent and empty face. It will not be full of liquid which would warp the drying wood.

Observing and, more importantly, feeling the Moon in this manner will give you the opportunity to hear her, to actually listen to her vibration. This phenomenon is called *Coyolxauhqui*, keeper of the original sound. *Coyol* is a necklace of dried nuts that can make a low level rattling sound. *Xauh* means "adorned with." *Qui* means "one who keeps." The ancients believed that the creation of the universe began through sound. In a creation story, when there was nothing except emptiness and silence, *Huehuecoyotl* (Old Coyote) cracked the silence by blowing his conch shell. The echo of that sound still permeates the cosmos. They also perceived that the Moon kept the vibration of the echo of Old Coyote's conch shell and that it is still possible, under the proper circumstances, to hear the sound of Creation's beginning. It is said that at the moment of getting pregnant, if she is attentive, a woman can hear the Moon's echo, confirming the creation of a new life.

The Seasons

The beginning of each season, which is actually a transitory position when Earth tilts between the tropic of Cancer and tropic of Capricorn as it orbits the Sun, is another opportunity to stop for introspection. Let us understand that as Earth transitions from Winter to Spring or Summer to Fall, our bodies are undergoing a similar transit. If, along with our daily greeting of the Sun, we face the first day of Spring, our bodies are also going from a Winter-like state into a renewal. As Earth enters Summer, we too move from a season of fertility to a season of solar strength. Fall is a slowing down period and Winter is a time of hibernation. We need not completely stop in Winter or go full steam in Summer, but by being aware and honoring our internal state in relationship to our orbit around the Sun, we can invite our ever present silent, wise self to begin walking in step with the seasons.

The Aphelion, Perihelion, and Equihelions

We also know that Earth has four other orbital positions, an aphelion, perihelion, and two equihelions that come thirteen days after each season begins. During each one of these days, we can also take time to meditate on the significance of these points. The equihelions, when Earth is the same distance from the Sun thirteen days after the Spring equinox as it was thirteen days after the Fall equinox, embody balance complementing the seasons they follow. The first day of the Fall and Spring equinoxes divide that 24-hour period roughly in half, the same amount of day as there is of night. This can be another reminder to be aware and maintain our internal and external balance.

The perihelion is when Earth is closest to the Sun. We can visualize this as the Sun exercising maximum pull on Earth as if wanting to bring her into his embrace. Think about your relationship with those you love and depend on. Ponder the dire consequences of Earth being completely embraced by the Sun. We would all burn up. No matter how close we are to a person, place, or idea, there must be a healthy space between us that we hold dear.

The aphelion is when Earth is farthest from the Sun. We can visualize this as Earth exercising her maximum strength to pull away from the Sun. Ponder the possibility of Earth detaching from the Sun's orbit. We would all freeze. This is a good time to meditate on our interdependency with others. How much of a distance do we want to set between us and those to whom we are closest?

Thirteen days after the Spring equinox, the equihelion position provides a unique opportunity for long term tracking of where we are in our lives. Every eight years, thirteen days after the Spring equinox, Venus aligns with the seven star cluster of the Pleiades. The last alignment was in April 3, 2004, and then 2012. During this time, the Pleiades align with Venus as Evening (*Tezcatlipoca*) and Morning Star (*Quetzalcoatl*). That is how the ancients discovered that the Evening and Morning Stars are one, after its evening disappearance Venus reappears under the Pleiades in the early morning.

Observing this phenomenon is a good reminder of how something that appears divided is actually one: earth and sky, night and day, light and dark, positive and negative, energy and matter, physical form and spirit, left and right brain—opposites are parts of a single whole. Likewise, we are one with Creation. The number of stars in the Pleiades cluster is symbolic of the seven portholes of our head through which we absorb information. As Venus aligns, seven becomes eight in which information becomes knowledge. Knowledge applied can become wisdom.

Cygnus: The Tree of Life

Another sky meditation can be practiced on August 12th and 13th when there is a meteorite shower. Because of our vantage point, the meteorites appear to fall on the constellation Cygnus, a six star constellation that looks like a cross. The ancients viewed this constellation as the Tree of Life which the Maya identified with the ceiba tree and the Aztecs with a cactus plant. When the calendar was developed by both cultures, they agreed to add another meaning to Cygnus, that of a corn plant. Hence the meteorites "falling" over Cygnus take on a double meaning. One is that the meteorite shower represents the watering of the Tree of Life. Another is that the meteorites are corn seeds being planted and sprouting into corn stalks. August 13, 3117 B.C. was assigned as the birth date of the Age of Corn. This is a good time for watering our souls, our lives, and planting new thoughts and goals.

Watching and using the night sky for meditation can be quite effective. Hunbatz Men, a Mayan elder from Yucatan, Mexico, recommends laying on your back and looking directly into the heavens avoiding any peripheral images to interfere with your focus. Given a good spot, you can actually feel as though you are in outer space itself blending your thoughts with the stars. You do not need to understand astronomy to meditate, just stare at the night sky, let go, and see what happens.

CHAPTER FOUR: Seven Practices

"Wisdom begins through a dialogue with your own heart."
Toltec proverb

We are born complete, but we forget. Much of learning is remembering. During our first season, we develop an intimate relationship with water. We are able to grow within the liquid that fills our mother's womb. We are comfortable moving in water. We are so comfortable, in fact, that at birth we know how to swim. But unless we continue our practice, we soon forget and have to take swimming lessons. It is the same with breathing.

Every infant instinctively knows how to breathe. Watch a baby's tummy and you can tell the air is going in deep as the lower belly rises and falls. Our fire within needs air and we are born being able to fully feed that fire. But as we grow older, our breathing becomes shallow and we take in air only for the lungs and not for the lower part of our body where, according to the ancients, we have an "internal furnace" out of which flows our *atlachinolli*, one of our four animating forces. Correct breathing is one of the seven things we have to re-learn in order to be able to live 104 years. The other six activities we need to learn and practice are how to eat, move, feel, think, share, and use water.

AIR: Breath

Every breath we take needs to be deep, going all the way to where the *atlachinolli* originates. At first, we must do this consciously, on a daily basis, and enough times so that we do it without thinking about it. The start is simple. Use the muscles of your lower belly with each breath to make the air go deep, not just to your lungs. Breathe in and out through your nose, avoid using your mouth. Taking in air with the mouth is useful only when you want to cool your internal fire, usually to offset an imbalance such as pain, hyperactivity, or high blood sugar. Adding an exercise program to this endeavor, especially tai-chi, chi-gong, and yoga will be of great help.

WATER: The Flow of Life

Most of us know of the medical recommendation to consume at least eight eight-ounce glasses of water daily. This gives our bodies the minimum requirement to maintain adequate hydration. Drinking up to thirteen would be an excellent practice. There is more to using water than drinking. Water is memory, living memory. Her perception of things around is profound. Drinking water that has been exposed to conflicting, hurtful circumstances becomes contaminated and that is what we are drinking. Therefore, take a moment to clear your mind before drinking and even make an effort to change your state of mind to a positive one. In other words, bless the water.

We use water for cleansing our bodies daily. Those of us who live in industrialized societies are used to taking a hot shower in the morning and we begin by dousing our heads. Neither practice is conducive to good health. This unnaturally heated water shocks the body and causes imbalances. It is best to shower or bathe in room temperature water and encounter this life-giving substance in its more natural state. Also, begin at your feet and gradually work your way up, with the head being the last one to get wet. Before you let the water go beyond your feet, wet your hand and rub your ear lobes. Then wet your hand again and rub some water on the top of your head where your fontanel used to be. This prevents the cold of the water from creating an imbalance. When someone splashes you with cold water you also get a shock, creating an imbalance, and opening your body to infection. When experiencing this, quickly wet your ear lobes with the cold water and then wet the top part of your head.

Water is cleansing in many ways. Simply keeping a bowl filled with water somewhere in your dwelling will provide a vibration-cleansing to your home provided you empty and fill the bowl on a regular basis. We recommend you keep water contained for this purpose for a maximum of seven days. A bowl of water is also good for meditation or what is called "water gazing." Sit holding the bowl in your hands over your lap. Head bowed, look straight into the water and allow your thoughts to flow. You may wind up submerged into the cloudiness of the water or sometimes see images and experience insights.

Finally, there is a note about tears. This precious liquid is one way we express emotion; they help us to fully experience and benefit from our emotions. When we see someone crying, the usual protocol is to give them some tissue to wipe away their tears. This is not what Creation intended. Our tears need to wet our skin and dry there. Allowing our tears to dry upon our skin produces a chemical reaction that enhances our joy, if that was the reason for our tears, or healing from the hurt which made those tears flow.

NUTRITION: Diet

We are what we eat. In an era of processed and fast foods, it is indeed a challenge to eat healthy. Just the same, the availability of alternatives is also refreshing. We can choose organic, vegetarian, vegan, or macrobiotic to name a few.

Dietary supplement programs are also readily available. What this manual offers is a simple dietary plan consisting of foods called the "Seven Warriors."

Mesoamerican diet was based around seven foods: beans (*etl*), squash (*ayotli*), corn (*tlayolli*), chile (*chilli*), amaranth (*uactli*), agave (*metl*), and cactus (*nopalli*). As long as these are a regular part of the diet, you can include meat of any kind. However, in and of themselves, they are able to provide complete nutrition. Supplementing these foods were chia, cacao, papaya, mesquite, and tomato. Chapter Five in this manual will further explain the Seven Warriors and this diet.

MOTION: Exercise

Most of us climb stairs every day. We do not realize that the way we currently negotiate each step is harmful to our backs. A more natural way of climbing stairs is moving from side to side, the way a snake crawls across the ground. Narrow stairs need to be climbed sideways rather than straight up. Climbing stairs in a vertical direction hurts our backs and takes its toll over time.

Daily motion is essential and it is important to do it properly. By that, we mean learning to move naturally, with the ebb and flow of gravity and not against it. Our strongest muscles are in our thighs; that is where the support of our bodies needs to be anchored. We have designed a society in which our spines, one of the weakest parts of the body, play this role. Sofas, chairs, and mattresses are illusory items of comfort. When we sit, our knees should be above our hips with our buttocks holding us up. Chairs, where our knees wind up below our hips, are actually causing a strain on our backs without us realizing. Beds need to be hard not soft. The springy structure of the mattress forces the spine to hold the body throughout the night and makes the vertebrae susceptible to misalignment and eventually possible fractures. In the long run, sleeping on the floor is a healthier option. At the very least, please make sure your mattress is firm.

Walking seems like a natural activity. Surely we all know how to walk. Young children have a natural bounce to their walk. Like deep breathing, it is something they seem to lose with age. Many people walk with their knees almost locked, moving as if they had sticks for legs. Our legs are three jointed limbs with which we move as if in a smooth continual dance.

When we move, we must allow our entire body to participate in each movement. This coordination is present early in our lives, but we forget it. To regain our natural bounce and coordination is rather simple: dance and swim often. Dancing and swimming are leisure activities that also discipline and exercise the body towards better coordination. It does not matter if you dance salsa, country, or rock n roll. Make dancing an integral part of your life. Ancients all over the world developed exercise disciplines or dances to teach healthy body motion. Again, tai-chi, chi-gong, or yoga is highly recommended. The ancient Mesoamericans also left for us a dance system which is practiced by many groups in Mexico and the United States. The three, better known systems are: Danza Azteca, Matachines, and Capoeira. Any one of these is excellent for learning how to synchronize breathing and body motion.

EMOTION: Feelings

A human face with only 43 muscles is capable of producing 10,000 different facial expressions. This remarkable feat is indicative of the variety of ways we can project different emotions. Our emotions, whether of great joy or deep sorrow, are released from our souls and hearts. It is important that we not repress but express them appropriately, and also be aware of what it is we are feeling. Many of us would have a difficult time naming more than a handful of feelings. Lists vary, but currently there are names for over 100 emotions.

While many of us know about our IQ, Intelligence Quotient, we would be hard pressed to know our EQ, Emotional Quotient. As young children, we had no difficulty expressing how we felt. Growing-up became a school for learning how to hide feelings, which created EQ challenged individuals. When we honor our feelings through awareness, expression, and action, we honor and nurture our souls. Awareness is being able to know what you are feeling. Expression is allowing your body to manifest it. Action is doing what the feeling's presence is guiding you to do: send flowers, renew a friendship, pay a debt, or attend church for prayer, etc. Without the vitality of our souls, the other healthy activities are not enough to sustain a body for a hundred years.

Emotional health is a state of being comfortable with ourselves. From that awareness, expression and action will follow. In today's world "to become comfortable in our own skin," many of us will seek therapy, enter a twelve-step program, or take up a spiritual discipline. With the advent of "energy psychology" such as Psych-K, there are many avenues in which to learn how to positively direct our emotions. Here are two simple suggestions:

One: Find a place that still has some natural surroundings, a spot in a park perhaps. Make it your spot, a place where you can spend a little time each day or on a regular basis. Sit there and notice the vegetation, weather, and any animal presence—ants, bees, worms. Be mindful not to disturb anything but observe how nature changes. Vegetation will grow, dry, and wilt. Ants will make their presence at certain times and completely disappear at others. Notice the temperature changes, when the wind blows and in what direction, the effects of rainfall on the place. This is a meditation that engages Mother Nature, our universal teacher. Being with nature is a good way of relieving stress.

Two: Take some time and make a list of seven activities that nurture your soul. This takes some introspection about what constitutes your soul and what activities nurture it. Ask yourself what you do or would like to do for fun but do not limit this to activities that are only fun. Be specific in this introspection. If you list art, what kind of activity related to art? Part of nurturing your soul may be doing something you have not done before. A friend of mine put on her list attending church services of different faiths. Exposure to a variety of church traditions not her own became a very soul nurturing experience. Once you have your list, integrate those activities into your life. This list may be something that will be a part of nurturing your soul for the rest of your life.

It is said that *Quetzalcoatl* founded the *Toltec* civilization (around 870 AD) on the premise that we should "love and create beauty." In the *Nahuatl* language, *tlazo* means both love and beauty and is synonymous with the word precious. Remember that in the story from Chapter One, Deer suggested that the Creators hide the secret of life inside the human heart. The ancients realized that the key to any human endeavor is finding that secret, which is Love. The Mayan scholar, Domingo

Martínez Paredes confirmed this from his deathbed in 1986 when he said, "What is most important is Love, to do everything with Love. Love is what truly has value."

THOUGHT: Seeds of Reality

The ancients divided the realm of thought, which includes the brain, the heart, and our entire nervous system, according to the model of the four directions wheel. We are created and born with four innate powers of thought: intelligence (East), will power (South), memory (West), and wisdom (North). A human mind needs to continually travel the wheel of these four powers and be aware that each has an "enemy" and an "ally." Both are beneficial in that they teach us. The ally of intelligence is analysis (figuring things out). Its enemy is justification (justifying our actions even when wrong). The ally of will power is instinct (sensing a need to act); its enemy is hesitation (thinking too much, or becoming afraid). The ally of memory is introspection (looking within and taking inventory); its enemy is indulgence (wanting to repeat something pleasant despite its danger such as drug addiction). The ally of wisdom is observation (being able to detach from a situation in order to get a more objective perspective); its enemy is isolation (becoming too apart from others, not wanting to participate). Moving continually around this wheel of thought gives us an opportunity to know ourselves and "look before we leap."

Spiritual teachers like Buddha, Krishnamurti, and Eckhart Tolle tell us our brain is an instrument. The thoughts we produce there are meant to serve our daily living. Learning how to think means learning how to use our brains as a useful tool to better our lives. They warn us to carefully observe our thoughts because these can determine our destiny. Our thoughts are the seeds of reality.

COMMUNITY: Sharing

We are social creatures. Few of us want to be hermits. What keeps any community functional is our ability to share. On a macro level, we only need to look at our civilization to realize how wide a gap we allow between the rich and the poor. Two percent of the world's population controls more than half of the world's wealth. The problem is not so much political or economic. There are ample resources for all of Mother Earth's children. The problem is not knowing how to share. Sharing is a human trait we seem to practice naturally as young children, if we could only continue this trait as we grow.

Our fear of sharing rises out of our fear of others. We cannot lose this insecurity simply by wishing it away. The most effective way is to practice service to community. Khalil Gibran, in *The Prophet,* tells us that when we give of our wealth we give little, but it is when we give of ourselves that we truly give. Learning how to share begins with the giving of ourselves. When we share we let go of our insecurities. Through service we find why "it is in giving that we receive."

The health enhancing value of learning and practicing these seven skills provides the basis for living the 104 years Creation intended for us. It is important to remember that we need to relearn how to breathe, eat, move, feel, think, share, and use water. Take time to reflect on the seven skills necessary to live your Nine Seasons of Life.

CHAPTER FIVE: Seven Warrior Foods

"The doctor of the future will no longer treat the human frame with drugs, but rather will cure and prevent disease with nutrition."
Thomas Edison

Over five thousand years ago, the people of central Mexico decided that the night when meteorites shower the sky (giving the appearance of rain falling over the glowing Cygnus constellation) would be the Age of Corn's birth date. Today, we know that date as August 12th. Long before that, they had made a covenant with a thistle-like plant called *Teocentli* so that she would transform in a way that would feed the People. Circumventing a normal evolutionary process, literally from night to day, this plant changed to produce large cobs of grain they called *Tlayolli*, Life Giver. In transforming, *Teocentli* lost her ability to self reproduce, so the People agreed that, henceforth, they would always plant her seeds. In this way, both species would survive.

Corn is an amazing produce. It came in four basic colors: red, white, yellow, and black. Blends of those colors then gave us others like blue, purple, green, and brown. Its vibration frequency is very close to the frequency of humans, providing a factual element to the Mesoamerican legend that humans were made from corn. Cooked, it is an excellent source of dietary fiber, thiamin, and folate. Raw, it is a good source of vitamin C, magnesium, and phosphorus. Today, corn, also known in Mexico by its indigenous names of *teocintli* and *maiz*, provides nutrition for the entire planet. Originally, it was part of the "Seven Warriors," a group of foods around which the Mesoamerican diet was organized.

Maiz (corn), Ayotli (squash), Etl (beans)

These seven warriors can be visualized as a food pyramid, with corn being at the top; the next tier is composed of beans and squash; followed by the third level which consists of amaranth, maguey (agave), chile, and cacti. The first three, along with water, provide the minimum nutrition a person needs. In other words, someone can live on corn, beans, and squash an entire lifetime. Although it is a plant based diet, it does not mean that you must be vegetarian. What is important is that no matter what else you add, they ought to be a regular part of our nutrition.

Among indigenous populations north of Mexico, corn, beans, and squash are known as the three sisters. Like in the south, they are planted together to help each other grow. The large squash leaves cover the soil and help retain moisture for her sisters. The corn stalk provides a means through which the bean vine can curl around and hold herself up.

The bean vines tie the corn stalks together against wind storms, and their roots make nitrogen for the maize roots. Once they wilt and dry, mixing them into the ground provides an excellent way of fertilizing the soil. As corn began traveling from central Mexico throughout the continent, this method of farming followed. Indigenous communities across north and south of the Americas planted the three sisters in the same manner.

It is said that the three sisters draw their power from their connection to three stellar bodies. Corn represents the Sun and is said to contain his power because it was the Sun who in the original covenant allowed the plant to transform sunlight into corn kernels. That is why corn contains all the colors of the sky.

Squash is a plant which represents the Moon because of her womb-like shape. To this day, the best time to plant squash is during the waxing Moon crescent because, at that time, the Moon is shaped in the form of a womb.

The vine which grows beans is symbolic of the motion of Venus around the Sun, particularly when Venus aligns between Earth and Sun and appears to streak across the Sun's surface. As we consume the three sisters, we honor their relationship to the heavens and ponder that we are ingesting the power of the Sun, Moon, and Morning and Evening Stars.

As with all the seven warriors, the key to their nutrition is eating the variety of meals that can be prepared from each one. Corn can be tortillas, bread, tamales, soup, popcorn, roasted corn- on-the-cob, cooked grains, or cracked corn mush. The corn plant produces a fungus called *huitlacoche* which can be cooked and served as a dip or as an additive to tacos. Squash can be steamed, fried, baked, or eaten raw. Her flowers can also be picked and cooked or eaten raw. Beans can be cooked whole, mashed, or fried. They can be served hot, cold,or as a salad additive. It is simple to neutralize the gas producing effects of beans by cooking them with an herb called *epazote,* easily found in most Mexican food markets. Bay leaves may be used for the same purpose.

Metl (maguey or agave)

The maguey plant is considered the General of this army of warriors because of its resistance to harsh environments, being able to grow even in places with little rainfall. Many of us know maguey as the plant from which tequila is made, but this plant produces a highly nutritional honey (*meoctli*) whose glycemic value makes it useful for diabetics. The Maguey also grows a long stem called *quiote*. Peel and sliced it can be cooked with a texture much like potato. Salted and prepared with other vegetables or meats, it makes for a delicious and healthy meal. Maguey roots have medicinal value used in the treatment of arthritis of the joints. This plant is a general of the warriors, but she is a female general. Maguey, part of the agave family, is the Moon's representative on Earth. Her spirit, *Meyahuel*, is said to be one of the two Earth female forces that renew the soil and transform the Sun's power into the season of Spring. The other female force is called *Tlazolteotl*, Earth's ability to convert decaying matter into fertilizer.

Nopal (cactus)

While the Maya associated the ceiba tree with the constellation Cyngus, the Aztecs gave this role to the nopal or cactus plant. This "Tree of Life" produces fruit called tunas, which grow in a variety of colors depending on their environment. Their sweetness also depends on the soil but they are meant as an appetizer or desert and not to be consumed in large quantities, as they are full of seeds that can cause constipation. The green sections, nopalitos, need to be cleared of thorns, then diced, and boiled just enough to become tender. This juice is usually strained and the cooked portions are stir fried with another food such as egg. The cactus juice can be used raw to mend wounds or as an additive to soaps or perfumes. The liquid inside a cactus branch has insulin-like properties and many people suffering from type-one diabetes use it to lower their glucose level.

Chilli (chile)

One chile pod has five times the vitamin C content of an orange. Its spiciness and chemical composition not only strengthen the body's immune system but also help the blood to circulate and improve digestion. There are over forty varieties of chile, and this indigenous cultigen comes in many colors, including orange and black. Chile can be eaten raw, cooked, stuffed or dried to create powder or sauces.

Huactli (amaranth)

Amaranth was actually outlawed by the Spaniards. The leaves are more nutritious than spinach. Its seeds are equally valuable in their nutrition. These seeds are also associated with the Winter Sun; they were previously used to form a doll which represented the "baby sun" being born in Winter. Because it was used in this manner, the Spaniards outlawed the plant along with the Sun ritual. They considered native rituals pagan and against the Catholic faith. Along the border in the states of Texas, New Mexico, and Arizona, there grows a plant that is part of the amaranth family called *kelite*. Considered as useless, many farmers see it as a weed, but many families use it as a healthy food source. While amaranth has a reddish color, this cousin is mostly green with streaks of red underneath the leaves.

Mesoamerican diet included a wide variety of foods, but it was organized around the seven warriors for two reasons. The combination of these foods can sustain a human being with excellent nutrition. Someone could eat only these foods for the rest of their life and all that would be needed is water. The addition of what some have termed "super foods" such as chia, papaya, avocado, and tomato along with seafood and deer or buffalo meat would compliment an already excellent diet. The other reason for the effectiveness of the Seven Warriors is that their integration creates the proper balance of approximately thirty percent blood acidity and an alkalinity of seventy percent.

Our ancients asked permission from a plant when cutting any part of it and begged forgiveness from an animal they killed for food. We believe it is good to include some kind of ritual or blessing to show our gratitude to the plants and animals we eat today. A meal is a prayer, meditation, and social gathering. It is a time for sharing with ourselves and others the power of Earth's vibrations woven into the fabric of fruits, vegetables, meats, and liquids. As we have mentioned before, nothing is better to motivate any sharing than that special power of the Universe placed in the center of our heart: Love.

CHAPTER SIX: Journey Through the Womb

"Our worst fear happens at the moment we are conceived to be in this world. All that remains after that is love and an adventurous quest for beauty."
The Warrior's Code

Our origin is not our parents. To paraphrase Khalil Gibran in *The Prophet*, we came through them, not from them. Our beginning is in the Infinite. The totality of Creation (*Teotl*) began there. How this is possible is an unanswerable question called "The Great Mystery." The truth of this principle of Creation can be found within ourselves and empowers us to exercise our role and responsibility in procreation. Conception occurs in the realm of the Infinite. While a couple may choose the act of intimacy, it is the Great Mystery that decides if their Love will be the beginning of another Life. This principle helps us nurture an attitude about the mystery and the sacredness of Life.

Our journey through the womb also has nine seasons consisting of five special events and the four spaces of time in between. Knowing when these special events occur and participating in them is important for nurturing a healthy, happy child. This participation also creates the conditions to actualize a life span of 104 years. A life developing in the womb is capable of receiving stimuli beyond the nutrition provided through the mother. The same science of biology that decoded the human genome tells us that every cell has the capacity to receive and record information via the stimulus of its membrane. This receptivity can have physical and emotional consequences. Our universal design is to be free of disease and psychological trauma. However, being unaware of the importance of the time in the womb can have detrimental consequences during pregnancy and after.

One, Nesting: 1 x 13 =13 days

After conception, the new human life attaches to the womb. This begins the process of nesting: the construction of the placenta, umbilical cord, and amniotic sac which is the housing in which the child will be formed. It is when this attachment occurs that a woman becomes pregnant. Most conceptions, for unknown reasons never attach. The vast majority of unions between sperm and egg do not achieve conception. Knowing this helps us accept the role of the Great Mystery. The decision to procreate life is connected to a power beyond us.

Across the centuries in the early morning sky several hours before dawn, there appears intermittently an alignment that the ancients recognized as a metaphor for the principle of conception in the womb. This celestial alignment, known as *Tlecuautlacuepa* (Returning Eagle of Fire), has no fixed cycle, so it's very difficult to predict its appearance. Those of us lucky enough to have seen it shed tears at that moment. The photo we have included does not do the actual sighting or experience justice (fig. 7). Venus appears just off to the side of the crescent Moon. The star dust falling at that time of the morning creates a veil between the Morning Star and the Moon, a white veil that is the outline of a woman. John Tarness, a Shoshone Medicine Man from Wyoming who showed us this phenomenon, explained that the crescent Moon is the womb; the woman is our Universal Mother through which all life forms enter our plane of existence; and the Morning Star is the touch of the Infinite, the Great Mystery, the only power that can make Life possible.

44

Fig. 7 Crescent Moon and Venus

Stardust falling on the crescent Moon

In the way of the ancients, women honor and celebrate nesting thirteen days after the attachment. When a mother-to-be keeps her rhythm with the Moon and learns to feel the internal cycles of her body (as discussed in Chapter Three: Sky Meditations), she knows immediately when attachment happens and is pregnant. For us in these times, it will take practice to relearn how to reconnect to the Moon and other creative forces of Mother Nature. Waiting thirteen days probably gives her a sense of security in the pregnancy and provides a way of calculating the arrival of the other remaining special events.

We suggest honoring the nesting by constructing a small nest or basket. Then the couple, family, and even members of the community come together and celebrate this construction. Everyone holds it and puts their good thoughts into the nest. The experience of the mother-to-be during this celebration will be transmitted with positive effects to the cells of the beginning human life.

Two, Heart: 4 x 13 = 52 days

After nesting, one of the major tasks of the gestation process is the heart and its vessels. This process peaks at 52 days. Our ancients describe this moment as the time when the *teyolia* or heart-spirit penetrates the center of this organ literally giving it a life of its own. Remember that this is where the "secret of life" was hidden upon Deer's suggestion. Day 52 of pregnancy can be celebrated with an event that recognizes the ability of this future human being to experience and give Love. We suggest a gathering that ends with the mother or father placing a small bright colored feather symbolizing the heart-spirit into the basket previously constructed. As the basket goes around, everyone in attendance can deposit a thought or a symbol of love into the basket.

Three, Brain: 13 x 13 = 169 days

From the heart comes a period of forming the brain and nervous system. This event comes at an important time around 169 days in which a significant portion of the brain and its connections will be created over a relatively short period of seven days. Key to this development are the two eyes, the eye of reason whose information will go into the left brain and the eye of knowing whose information will go into the right brain. This separate perception of the environment and its montage (composite) inside our brains is the dominant process that feeds our thinking for the rest of our lives. The purpose of understanding this is not for choosing to be a left or right brain dominant individual but to integrate our reason (logic, quantification, sequencing) with our knowing (intuition, artistic sense, wisdom).

To celebrate this occasion and help our future daughter or son achieve this integration, we suggest that those attending participate in a game of symmetry with the future mother. Trace a large circle on an 11" by 17" sheet of paper with a line through the middle. As the mother-to-be draws a figure on one side, have another person attempt to make the same drawing on the opposite half of the split circle (fig. 8). The future mother might have a specific figure in mind or just let the design flow with the game. Make it fun and perhaps have everyone participate in coloring or painting the overall figure produced.

Other activities to consider are coloring or painting a drawing of a mandala. Tibetan designs are especially detailed and intriguing. You also could simply trace your hands crossing at the thumbs forming a two headed bird, the hands symbol for Venus as Morning Star and Evening Star discussed in Chapter One under "eight are the birds." After forming the figure, paint each hand a different color. These activities emphasize a combination of perception with symmetry. Use your imagination. Remember that learning how to think is one of the seven activities for living 104 years.

Fig. 8 Symmetry Exercise

**An example of the symmetry exercise
for the 169th day of pregnancy**

Four, Soul: 20 x 13 = 260 days

A momentous event occurs in the womb at 260 days: the development and emergence of what we will later call our soul begins. Cuddled within the fontanel, the opening at the crown of our head, there will appear a small radiant sphere the ancients called *tonally* which literally means "solar vibration." As we explained in Chapter Two, this is one of the four animating forces of our body. The other three are the *teyolia,* the spirit at the center of our heart; the *ihiyotl,* which directs our passions that are stored in our liver; and the *atlachinolli,* the life force that flows out of our bladder. Over the next thirteen days, these animation forces will begin working together.

The *tonalli* contributes to our ability to move and provides a direct connection between us and the Sun. This is our solar being and consciousness, or what the ancients defined as the soul. It is said that upon our death our body returns to the Earth, our spirit to Creation, and our soul to the Sun.

A fitting activity to celebrate receiving our solar vibration at 260 days would be to experience a sunrise from a geographic location where the horizon can be clearly seen. Watch the slow emergence of the Sun as it gradually eliminates the stars from sight and returns the landscape to its full color. This might make a nice family outing which can include members of the community. As the Sun rises, the mother-to-be can bare her belly to the sunlight and rub her baby with the solar energy from the 260th day's first light.

Five, Body: (20 x 13) + 13 = 273 days

At 260 days, a human body is physically complete inside the womb. We are not born at that time because our animating forces need thirteen days to connect and begin a process of integration. Once the four forces have cemented their initial connections, we lose our ability to breathe inside a sac of amniotic fluid and stop being a "fish." Now the water breaks. This last phase completes the Nine Seasons in the Womb (fig. 9). This sacred moment is considered to be very personal and private. Ancients believed only women were able to handle and assist the pregnant woman deliver her child. As much as we respect Tradition, we believe it can be a very special moment for mother and father.

Our only suggestion within the context of this manual directly related to the birth of the child is for the parents to have made a decision about two important parts of this life giving process: the umbilical cord and placenta. It is important they not be discarded but stay with the parents as an offering to Mother Earth in any way they deem most appropriate. The placenta can be dried and kept in powder form. This organ was the child's third mother besides his or her human mother and Mother Earth. The umbilical cord was the baby's lifeline through which nutrition, emotion, and much of the mother's Love flowed. Traditionally, the umbilical cord is buried in a place that will remain as the child's Earth- center, his or her place of origin. Many still bury the umbilical cord in a special place.

Fig. 9 Nine Seasons in the Womb

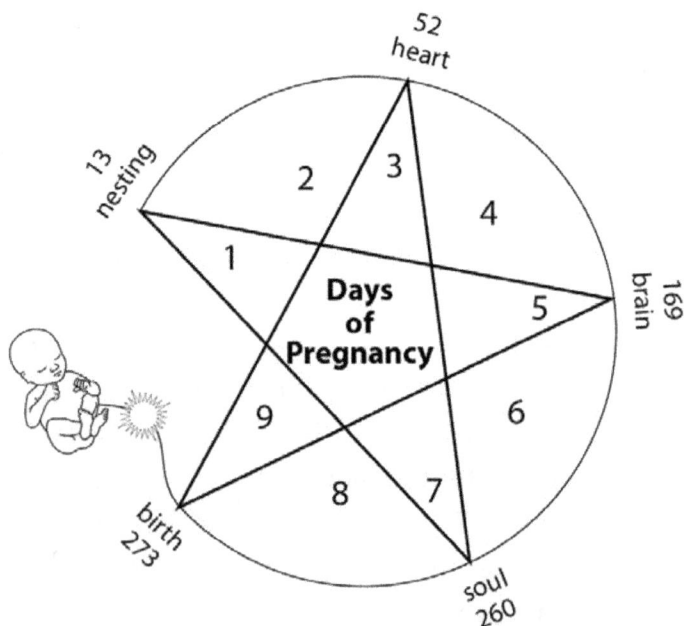

The pentagram is a useful form because it is the shape of the human body: four limbs and one head

CHAPTER SEVEN: Keeping Count of Our Seasons

*"To everything there is a season, and a time
for every purpose under heaven."*
Book of Ecclesiastes

We are born complete. Our authentic selves know we are equipped to live a long life in the way Mother Creation's love intended. The concept of the "perfectible human" assumes we arrive deficient. Any defects of our personality and body are self created, not imposed by the Universe. When we return to our authentic selves, we can employ our innate abilities and allow the Mother Creation's Love to do her work. This manual is meant to be used in this way. In this journey, each of us takes responsibility for ourselves by carrying out the tasks that maintain our authenticity and also by being responsible for assisting others.

Every seven years our body completes a renewal. It is as if we get a new body every seven years. Every thirteen years we complete an even greater transformation. The ancients tell us we are born with the capacity to renew our body thirteen times and undergo the greater transformation seven times (7 x 13 = 91). Thus, we have the ability to renew our bodies all the way up to age 91. After that, we can still live at least thirteen years more. How we maintain this capacity is what this manual is also about.

In Chapter One, we explained in the *cuenta* "Nine Are the Seasons" that our lives can be divided into two parts. The first 52 years are our receiving years and the final 52 years are our giving years. Each of the two phases has four seasons giving us eight seasons. Counting the time in the womb as another season gives us a total of nine seasons of life. In each one, we undergo critical developmental changes. Awareness of when and what happens during each season gives us the ability to participate in the nurturing of a life spanning 104 years.

Nine Seasons of a Human Life

- Womb

- Zero to 13 years: Childhood

- 13 - 26 years: Adolescence to maturity

- 26 - 39 years

- 39 - 52 years

- 52 - 65 years

- 65 - 78 years

- 78 - 91 years: becoming and elder

- 91 - 104 years: learning our death song

Season One: Zero to 273 Days

We have already explained that our first season is in the womb, a time consisting of five special events and the four spaces between them. Of course, everything that happens in the womb is special. Please understand that this is just a model intended to guide our participation with procreation. In reviewing what happens in the womb, we are including the other "special" events between the five. They occur over a period of time rather than at a specific number of days.

- At thirteen days of pregnancy, the embryo is fully attached and creating its nest.
- During the first 52 days, the embryo chooses what sex it will be.

- At 52 days the *teyolia* enters the center of the now fully functioning heart.

- After 52 days, the *teyolia* undertakes the role of extending the heart into a nervous system and a brain. The *heart* creates the brain. Thus, it is the heart that is meant to guide our actions.

- At 169 days, the body forms most of the brain during an accelerated period of seven days.

- The heart, brain, and nervous system conduct an electromagnetic flow throughout the body. Out of this electromagnetism, the *tonalli* and the *atalchinolli* and its meridians will be formed.

- At 260 days, the *tonalli* appears on our fontanel.

- The *tonalli, teyolia, atlachinolli, and ihiyotl* begin connecting and working with each other.

- At 273 days, a child is born. Remember that right after birth is an excellent opportunity to help the child keep their ability to swim. This will help in the transition to walking.

Season Two: The First Thirteen Years

During this time, we undergo important changes. In the first two years, the *tonalli* will fully submerge into the skull and the fontanel will close completely. The first physical manifestation of the *tonalli* blending with the body will be the growth of our first teeth. The second manifestation will be our ability for speech. In this period of the first season, it is recommended to keep the child close and physically pressed to the parents, being touched and caressed often and made to feel welcome in every possible way. Positive reinforcement cements a good personality. At this time a child's third eye is completely open and will be able to see the auras of those around and visually experience their internal mental state. If someone becomes angry, the child will see the color red flare around them and flames shooting from their eyes.

Between the ages of two and four, a child first experiences being independent from the parents. At this time, the *tonalli* and *atlachinolli* begin the process of creating more versatile movements of the human body. It is a good time to engage the child in games that involve a lot of movement, especially dancing. We need to help their observation and practice of flexibility and motion.

From age four to seven is the period appropriate for playful instruction. This is the time adults describe children as being "sponges" when it comes to learning. This is the prime opportunity for them to learn more than one language. Exploration and experimentation, especially with art, is the key to learning. Discovery becomes their greatest stimulus. Although our current educational system rejects this notion, now is not the time for formal instruction in reading and writing other than what they can do out of their own interest and curiosity. Reading to them and modeling writing to them is no problem, but forcing them to do it interrupts the integration of the three animating forces and distorts the personality Mother Creation's Love intends for us. Learning mathematics is quite appropriate for this stage. As math is a natural language, children are able to grasp simple mathematical concepts (like addition and subtraction) to more complex mathematical concepts such as geometry. The children who attend Waldorf Education schools have no problem with early introduction of mathematics while delaying formal reading and writing instruction until age ten.

From the age of seven until adolescence is a time to create art more formally and construct models in which they apply what they learn. The geometry learned earlier can now be applied more concretely to the design and formation of architectural structures. This is the time to begin presenting math word problems that gradually become reading and penmanship assignments. This is an excellent time to begin identifying emotions and open dialogues reflecting upon their artwork, science projects, home life, and ideas about career choices. By respecting and working with the natural seasons of life, the child will develop into an excellent reader and writer before age eleven. The child will also develop a good foundation to tackle what can be the very trying season of a teenager.

Season Three: Adolescence

Around age thirteen, the animating forces will reach into the liver and bring in the force that generates our passions. Housed there are all our emotions related to our instinctual fight or flight response. Focused tasks and their completion reinforce our confidence. If there is such a time when we need Love, it is during adolescence. The ancients considered the sexual drive produced during this season too powerful and usually required adolescence to be a time for marriage. The percolating of sex drives and psychological insecurities makes room for a time of "natural" neurosis that begins to settle around age 21 (during the third renewal of our physical body). By age 26, we have not only finished constructing our soul, the personality we will employ the rest of our lives, but we are also creating our first family and focusing on our children.

Season Four: Ages 26 through 39

Between the ages of 26 and 39, we are in our fourth season, during which time we help our children enter their own adulthood. This is an excellent time to change habits or incorporate new traits. The ancients remind us that the *Quetzalcoatl* who founded the Toltec Civilization began this awesome task at age 26 after leaving the Mesoamerican monastery of *Xochicalco* located in Morelos, Mexico.

Season Five: Ages 39 through 52

At age 39, we enter the final stage of our *Tezcatlipoca* or "receiving" half of Life. It is time to take inventory of how much we have accumulated and what we are lacking. Our goal here is that at 52 we are ready to become servants of the community and let go of our "receiving" or *Tezcatlipoca* years and embrace our *Quetzalcoatl* or "giving" years.

Season Six: Ages 52 through 65

At age 52, our life's orientation begins to shift towards community service. We are preparing to become elders, a time in which we will be trusted for crucial advice. We begin detaching from our family and deepening our roots to the greater community. If we are male, our feminine side begins to strengthen and vice-versa with females.

Season Seven: Ages 65 through 78

At age 65, we begin our preparation for the greatest responsibility of all—the authority of an elder. We think of authority in indigenous communities as the chief, but, as it was well phrased in the film set in the Brazilian jungle, *The Emerald Forest*: "When a chief tells others what to do, he stops becoming chief."

Season Eight: Ages 78 through 91

At age 78, we enter our eighth season, now as an elder. Here we are of service through a position of authority. In traditional communities, the council of elders had veto power over all decisions. The ancients say that by this season we ought to have mastered the colors red and black. The image of red and black, side by side, is a metaphor for wisdom. Black is the color of illusion and red the color of truth. A wise person can walk along a red path while having the black path laid out close to his or her side.

Season Nine: Ages 91 through 104

At age 91, we are still elders but begin searching for or practicing our death song. It's said that those that follow the Natural Way can decide the time of their death. For them, it is like going to sleep and never waking up. Pablo Choc Bac, a young Mayan from Guatemala, described for us such an event:

My uncle was a Mayan priest serving our community. He was old, over ninety. One day he said, "It is time to say farewell." He prepared himself for ceremony for about a week. We all attended the ceremony. That evening, he went to sleep and died peacefully during the night.

Grouping the Days

To get into the rhythm of your seasons, age does not matter. Determine what season you are in and ponder how much of that reality is true for you. We are not going to live our lives season by season just for today.

Calculate how many days you are from your birthday. Living the *Tonalpohualli*, the solar count of the Aztec Calendar, is done in groups of thirteen. Your birthday is day zero. After your birth date, keep track of twenty groups of thirteen days. Every thirteen days undergo some kind of cleansing, preferably a fast. After undergoing twenty cleansings, you will have lived through one solar count of 260 days (related to Earth's orbit as discussed in Chapter Three and also the number of days it takes to receive the glowing sphere of your soul on your fontanel).

For thirteen days after a 260-day period, assign yourself a task that involves body coordination. Wood work, painting, learning a new dance, taking an emergency rescue course, a two week course in swimming, martial arts, or ballet. See the task through and celebrate. You will be at 273 days, the amount of time Mother Creation took to completely form you in the womb.

Start the process of doing a cleansing every thirteen days; only this time you will undergo seven cleansings (7 x 13 = 91 days). This puts you at 364 days, one day before your birthday. Remember that back in the womb this was your last day as a fish. Make this day a time to renew your relationship with water. Find a natural body of water and spend a good part of this day there. If there is a rainstorm and it is not too cold, go for a walk through the rain and get soaking wet. Do some research and find out from what aquifer the water you use comes from. This may be an especially good time to do water gazing.

Find a way to be grateful to Mother Earth for her precious liquid. Consciously reacquainting yourself with this source of life is a form of preparation to be born again. After celebrating your birth(day), begin the cycles of thirteen days again, integrating the other information provided in this manual. We were made to have a good birth, a good life, and a good death.

CHAPTER EIGHT: The Nine Challenges to a Good Death

"Can this be true? We live here forever for just one brief moment."
Netzahualcoyotl, 1470

We remain alive because our cells are continually dying and making way for new cells. Life being sustained by death is a process well known to the ancients, who understood that the practice of a good death is an important part of having a good life. They thought of life as a dream and death as waking up. We come from the Infinite and to our origin we shall return. Everyone is born with this destination. How we get there is part of learning how to create for ourselves a long fulfilling life and then entering the "tenth season" in a joyous embrace of the Infinite. Fear not death, rather love Life accepting all its transitions and realize we are eternal but not permanent.

Resisting the natural changes of life can create fear and suffering. Know that our spirit is the force of the Great Mystery that initiates us into our present life. Upon death, that spirit will carry the memory of all we experienced on Earth. Our personality is not our spirit but a kind of computer program in our brain to create a temporary self to administer the mechanics of our body. It will cease to be when we die. As that programming begins to be dismantled, our fears arise and cause our brain to create false hopes or horrifying delusions. This only prolongs the suffering of having to surrender that which was never meant to last forever. Heaven and hell do not exist outside our own imaginings.

Death is not a single event but a threefold process. The first is when our body shuts down (sometimes due to physical trauma). This shutting down is more like a hibernation that can last several hours. The soul, the composite of electromagnetic forces that gives us animation, detaches while the body is in hibernation. This is the second part of the dying process. In the third and final part, the spirit, also the origin-spark of Life, departs leaving the body to stiffen and decompose.

Before the departure of the spirit, it is still possible to restore someone to life or spontaneously return after being pronounced medically dead. It is in our hibernation that the brain can use its power of thought to create delusions of heavenly pleasure or hellish pain. This is what we know as a near death experience. A body can be restored and a soul retrieved. However, once we surrender our spirit, death is final unless the Great Mystery intervenes.

Physical trauma is not necessary to enter the dying process. In the previous chapter, we gave the example of a Mayan priest who, after entering his ninth season of life, created his own death ceremony, invited his community, and then died peacefully during the night. Our return to the Infinite is meant to be a glorious transformative experience if we are prepared and do not let our temporary self get in the way. To help us prepare, the ancients created a meditation in the form of a story that presents nine challenges. After you have read and become familiar with the journey of nine levels, practice visualizing the journey. Practicing this meditation can help us surrender to the dying process.

There are similarities between the nine challenges of death and the nine stages in the womb. The first challenge is crossing a wide river aided by your soul. In the last two stages of birth, you receive a soul and then the water you have lived in for 273 days drains giving you no choice but to leave. In death, the second challenge is to cross two mountains crushing into each other. In birth, you must cross the birth canal which also tends to crush your body as you squeeze through. Just as you gradually receive your flesh, bones, and heart in the womb, they are removed with each challenge in death.

First Challenge: *Apanohuayo* (Crossing the Wide River)

Open your eyes. Throughout your life your heart has taught you the use of four powers (Courage, Endurance, Patience, and Love) to prepare you for this moment. You are ready. See before you the wide river you will cross. It is so wide you cannot see the other side. Its current is strong and will fight you, but you will be able to swim its entire width. Do not worry. Look down at your side. See the dog with a cotton string around his neck? He is *Xolotl*, the one who keeps and protects your soul. He will guide you across the river. Pet him as you once did your own pet. Let him lick you and rub against you. He knows who you are, but you must be sure of him. Grab and hold on to the cotton string around him, calmly walk into the water until there is no bottom to step on. Remember that before you were born, you knew how to swim. Trust yourself. Trust your dog. As both of you cross the river, you will realize *Xolotl* is your soul.

Second Challenge:
Tepe-monamiktia (Being Crushed by Mountains)

As you emerge from the river, your dog is no longer with you and your clothes have been removed. Take a close look at yourself. What you once covered, needs covering no more. Was there ever a need to feel shame for any parts of your body? Your soul has returned to a good place. Notice that you feel no heat or cold, only complete comfort. You are by yourself but do not feel alone. Ahead of you there are two mountains very close to each other. Walk between them and get to the other side. As you walk, they will continually crash into one another. As they do, they will also crush you but realize you will not be harmed. There will only be pain if you imagine it and your walk made more difficult. You may fall, but you will walk until reaching the other side. Remember, there is no more pain.

Third Challenge: *Itztepetl* (Obsidian Mountain)

Your body is now soft like cloth, yet you are still able to stand. You feel no pain. Now look at the next mountain just a few steps away. It is black and from here you can see the sharp edges protruding from its surface. They are blades of obsidian, knives you must try to avoid as you climb and cross it, but understand you will not be able to prevent all of them from cutting you. Walk across this mountain carefully. Each time you are cut by its edges, remember the sharp words with which you once wounded someone during your lifetime. You will not feel the pain of the cut, but your heart will feel the hurtfulness of your words. Shed tears as you are still able to cry. Continue until you have reached the other side.

Fourth Challenge: *Zehuecayan* (Across Snow Covered Hills)

Notice the cuts all over your body. Each one bleeds and parts of your flesh hang likes ribbons. Notice but do not dwell; there is no pain, no need to panic. Concentrate instead on the eight white hills in the distance. This is where you will find new strength. By the time you get there, you will be empty of all fluids. As you get close, you will experience a stinging cold enter each one of your wounds. Do not stop. As you cross these eight hills covered with snow, you will soon realize the cold is giving you a new vitality. With each hill, the cold will sharpen and so will your inner strength. You will want to run and be finished with your challenge. Stay calm and keep walking. The hills are far away and it will take you a long time to reach each one, cross each, and be finished with your challenge.

Fifth Challenge: *Itzehecayan* (Mountain of Obsidian Wind)

As you walk over the last snow-covered hill, you will encounter winds blowing with the strength you have not felt before. They will rip the ribbons of flesh off your body. They will disorient you and you will get so confused you will want to turn back. If you do, there will be nothing there but more wind. It will not matter which way you go, the wind will be against you. So keep walking and do not turn back. By now you will be able to see your skeleton begin to appear as your skin is peeling away. Again, notice there is no pain. Seeing your bones uncovered will be like recognizing your skeleton for the first time. Losing parts of your flesh will not have diminished your strength. Going against the sharp winds you realize a curious fact. You are not breathing. You no longer need air to gather your strength and move forward.

Sixth Challenge: *Temiminaloyan* (Rain of Arrows)

Upon being free of the razor-like winds, you now stand as a skeleton partly covered by flesh. You are close to having your true self revealed. To take a step closer to that realization, the rest of your flesh must go. As soon as you take one step forward, a rain of arrows descends upon you removing the last coverings of your skeletal self. As each arrow pierces you, remind yourself how painless each blow is. But because you still have the memory of pain, each arrow causes in you a hesitation and you will want to shield yourself from them. You can form a shield out of the kindness of your heart and temporarily keep the arrows from piercing you. But soon the shield will be gone and when the falling arrows stop, you will be ready for your next challenge.

Seventh Challenge:
Teocolehualoyan (Where Jaguars Eat Human Hearts)

Examine yourself carefully. You are now a skeleton. Every piece of flesh has been removed; all vessels of blood and fluids are gone; and no organs remain except one—your heart. It no longer beats. There is no more blood to pump but in your heart is the memory of all your feelings, especially of those you loved most. Suddenly there comes upon you *ocelotl*, the jaguar. Look at his dark spotted skin. As he attacks, you will want to use every ounce of your strength to protect yourself. But, realize that the jaguar is a good omen. He will break through your chest with his saber-like jaws, devour your heart, and then quickly leave. Look into the hole left behind. It is round and dark like the mirror *Tezcatlipoca*. There you can gaze at yourself and begin to realize who you really are. A sense of lightness now permeates your being, the opening in the middle of your chest begins to widen, and a sensation of sinking becomes overwhelming.

Eighth Challenge: *Apanuayo* (Lake of Dark Waters)

The opening through which the jaguar took your heart has become so wide as to engulf you completely. Nothing is left of you except the awareness of being deep within dark waters. Nothing you have ever experienced can compare to this complete silence, a fluidity of total stillness. This feels like eternity, but it is not. In the distance you hear a sound, as if someone is calling you. As you follow the voice you emerge out of the waters and see only a large, black reptile. Nothing else is visible. Everything around the reptile is neither light nor dark. Only the animal is visible. No matter where you look, right, left, up, down, behind, or even where you remember having a body, only the large reptile is present, repeating the same word: *Xochitonal* (Flowering Sun). With each repetition, you come closer to knowing who you are, have always been, and will continue to be: a flowering sun. No more words are needed. What you longed for, knowingly or unknowingly, all your life has been realized and you understand that now you must deliver the treasure of your essence to the Great Mystery. Gladly, you are ready to return what was given to you at the beginning of time.

Ninth Challenge: *Mictlan* (Dwelling Place of the Dead)

Water now returns in the form of nine rivers ending in waterfalls, each one dropping into the next. Through these nine waterfalls you flow until the final waterfall delivers you to *Mictlan*, the dwelling place of the dead. There you find *Mictlantecutli* and *Mictlancihuatl*, Father and Mother Death. They have been waiting for you. Upon meeting them, out of the memory of your lifetime comes a new understanding. You are delivering the treasure of your essence, the touch of the Great Mystery to them. It is the same treasure delivered to your Earthly parents when you were conceived. You are now giving to Father and Mother Death the same essence that created you. With this gift, even the keepers of Death will be Creators of Life.

Smiling, they tell you that your ordeals are over. You can finally sleep and dream. But you know there will always be another journey. As all of *Mictlan* becomes illuminated by the stars of the night sky to acknowledge your presence, you curl up into the hands of Mother and Father Death, humble servants of the Great Mystery. Perhaps in the next journey you will remember how Death and Life feed each other and that existence is endless beauty where every ending is a beginning.

Micailhuitl Xochimique:
Day of the Dead or Flowering of the Ancestors

On the first two days in November across Mexico and the southwestern United States, people set up altars to remember those who have gone before them. They place samples of the deceased one's favorite foods or items that belonged to them on their altars. Many visit graves, clean them, and leave offerings. Day of the Dead, as the occasion is called even though it involves two days, is the integration of two similar beliefs from different sides of the world. In Celtic Europe and ancient Mexico, there was a time set aside for people to give their ancestors an opportunity to return and be with them. November 1st is when the spirits of those who died as children return. On November 2nd, the adult spirits return. In this manner, the living receive nurturing and guidance from the dead.

Our spirit was part of the Universe before inhabiting our body and continues after we have completed our death journey. That spirit is not our personality or us as we were when alive. But our spirit carries the memory of our human experience. It is that memory which the ancient Celts and Mexicans made a space for once a year. They believed that by remembering those who had gone to the underworld, to *Mictlan,* it made a difference in someone being a spirit rather than a ghost. We get to come back, not as we were but as we have always been: Spirit.

CHAPTER NINE: The Seventh Generation

"If you reason and think soundly, no matter what path you follow in solving a problem, inevitably you arrive back at yourself."
G.I. Gurdjieff

Imagining the future is a useful exercise only if it can be an act of faith. Thinking about the future is counterproductive when we stir fear or attempt to see only projections of our own selfishness by dreaming of things that we were never meant to be. Some one hundred thousand years ago, it did not take the first human beings long to realize the miraculous complexity of Creation and the vulnerability of human desire to alter it.

Left unchecked, human beings can unleash the delusion that somehow we can improve on what has been divinely given; in doing so, we damage the web of Life to our own detriment. It is to our own peril because Creation will always correct her course and, in the process, eliminate the source of the problem. This book offers ways by which our ancestors dealt with that delusion. We conclude with a meditation the ancestors utilized to keep themselves from denying the Creator's paradise to future generations. It is known as the Lesson of the Seventh Generation.

When my children were born, I could not imagine them having children. But something happened when they finally did. I was able to imagine my grandchildren having children and that significantly changed my thinking. There was a feeling of urgency in my life I had not felt before. Ideals were no longer abstract goals. There was a need to make them more than lofty sentiments. My worry about what we humans were doing to Earth took on a reality that was startling.

Years before, I had been taught about the Lesson of the Seventh Generation, which teaches that any action that changes Mother Earth must be weighed against how it will affect our seventh generation. This teaching seemed simple enough, but after the birth of my grandchildren, I realized that applying it felt like an intangible exercise lacking practicality. Visualizing seven generations ahead did not seem honestly possible.

Time as a topic has been part of humanity since we began quantifying our existence. Our brains have a need and a knack for putting numbers to the motion of Creation, even such ephemeral concepts as time. Our sages have told us that "the measurement of time can be precise and long range, spanning thousands of years, but the measurement of time has nothing to do with its essence. Time in the measure sense does not exist" (Ernesto Briones, *Mayan Time*, 1974).

One of our indigenous calendars, the *Tonal Machiotl* or Aztec Sun Stone, illustrates a human face at the center anchored on each side by claws holding onto a heart, presumably human. This symbol is called *Kauitl*, which roughly translates as "time." However, it is not the measure of time, but rather the concept of being anchored in the present moment, which the modern day mystic, Eckhart Tolle, has called the Eternal Now. Motion across time is not a transition from past to future. Rather, it is a movement always occurring in the present. The past and future do not exist except as part of that never ending Now.

This may sound quite complex or mystical, yet it needs to be understood in its simplest form in order for the Lesson of the Seventh Generation to be grasped. This was the part I was missing when I would invoke this lesson and find myself only pretending to visualize the future seven lifetimes ahead.

The idea that measured time is not real is no longer a philosophical argument. Quantum physicists have confirmed this revelation in their experiments. Stephen Hawking, in "A Brief History of Time," introduced the idea to the general public. But, I am not a physicist, and my grasping of this concept came in the pedagogy of ceremony, perhaps the most useful activity left to us by our ancestors.

I was fortunate that a close friend, Peter Garcia, was able to use a ceremonial setting to explain this ancestral teaching. For the first time, it became practical knowledge. Peter is the offspring of a Mexican father and Hopi mother. He is younger than I but often has a deeper perspective about indigenous culture. He seemed the natural source for advice over my renewed concern about what Earth I was going to leave for my seventh generation.

"You have an unrealistic view of this teaching," Peter told me upon hearing me explain this ancient meditation. "It's extremely difficult for any human being to envision seven generations in the future. That's a misinterpretation."

He guided me to a new understanding; one that made sense because it gave me the ability to do as the lesson commands: weigh my actions against the interest of seven generations.

Our interaction on this matter occurred over the construction of an altar for a ceremony he was to conduct that evening. Peter has, among other spiritual charges, a Native American Church fireplace. He is a Road Man, more accurately a peyote priest, responsible for conducting all night ceremonies in which the sacred cactus (peyote) is used as a sacrament. Ceremonial and medicinal use of this plant can be documented on this continent as far back as ten thousand years.

The altar consists of a sand crescent mound pointing East, marking an area where a fire is kept through the night and where the ceremonial fire keeper spreads the red coals to eventually form an image—usually an eagle. In the middle of the mound sits a "chief" or dried peyote button, which embodies the Spirit of the Medicine and is said to be the one actually conducting the ceremony through the Road Man.

We had just finished the mound and Peter took the opportunity to use it to illustrate the meaning behind the seventh generation. He picked up a fist-sized stone and set it in place of the peyote chief. "This is you. Except the rock is a lot less ugly," he said jokingly.

Peter then took his staff and dug a line from the mound just below the rock to the left side of the crescent mound and also one to the right side. Then he made a central line ending at the spot where the fire was to be lit and kept.

"The left line represents your great grandparents," he told me. "The right line represents your grandchildren's children. The central line is still you. With me so far?"

Between the left line and the central line, Peter drew two equally spaced lines with his staff. He did the same between the central and right line. He obviously had practiced at drawing lines on the ground as they looked as if he had used a ruler to trace them. "I know you can count, but how many lines do we have now?" he asked.

There were seven lines radiating out from where the peyote chief sits. Even before Peter continued with his explanation, the practical meaning of the lesson of the seventh generation started to become clear to me. As soon as he said one line represented my great grandparents and the other my great grand children, a sensible way of visualizing seven generations began unfolding.

We are at the middle of generational space. To our left are our parents, grandparents, and great grandparents. To our right are our children, our grandchildren, and great grandchildren. When we undertake an action that changes our relationship with Creation, we look to the left and visualize ourselves in the place of our great grandparents and look across to our right and visualize our grandchildren's children. It is then that we are better able to realize how an action can affect seven generations.

No human being can see seven generations beyond themselves. It is simply not realistic. Peter explained that we need to be part of the sequence.

"We have to be one of the generations," he explained picking up the stone he had in place of the peyote chief. "We are the generation in the middle. From there we can see ourselves as any one of the other six. It is easier to visualize the parents of our grandparents and the children of our grandchildren that see seven times into the future. We *are* the seventh generation!"

He tossed the rock and laughed, "See? Now you've made me mess up my altar."

Index of Illustrations

Glossary

Acatl (a-ka-tl): Reed; one of the twenty days of the Aztec Calendar; also represents the years whose vibrations come from the Eastern Horizon.

Atlachinolli (a-tlah-chee-no-lee): An electromagnetic wave that acts like fire but moves like water and is centered at the base of the bladder.

Calli (Ka-lee): House; one of the twenty days of the Aztec Calendar; also represents the years whose vibrations are directed toward the Western Horizon.

Cipactonal (See-pahk-tonahl): Crocodile Sun; half of the pair of the parents of humanity, the original couple.

Coyolxauhqui (Co-yol-shau-key): The Sister of *Huitzilopochtli*; this name honors the time when a full Moon appears on the evening of the Winter Solstice and describes the Moon as keeper of the original sound of Creation.

Cuenta (Koo-en-tah): Counting a sequence, numerically ordered.

Cuento (Koo-en-toe): A fictional story, usually a fairytale, legend, or myth.

Huitlacoche (Wee-tla-ko-che): The original Nahuatl name is *Cuitlacochi*, sleeping manure; it is a dark blue edible fungus that grows on corn; *tacos de huitlacoche* are popular in central Mexico.

Huitzilopochtli (Weet-seel-opoch-tlee): Hummingbird Leaning Towards the Left; a name given to the Sun at the Winter Solstice when the Sun leans most to the Southern Horizon just as the human heart leans to the left.

Ihiyotl (Ee-hee-yotl): An electromagnetically charged greenish gas under the liver that activates human passions, the sex drive, and extreme emotions such as anger; an imbalance of these drives and emotions can damage the liver and pancreas.

Itzehecayan (Its-eheca-yan): *Itz* is obsidian; *echeca* is wind; *yan* is region; region where the wind cuts like obsidian blades.

Itztepetl (Its-the-pe-tl): *Itz* refers to obsidian, a glass like mineral used to make blades for delicate cutting; *tepetl* is a mountain; literally, "obsidian mountain"; mountain whose edge cuts like obsidian blades.

Maiz (mah-eez): The Taino (indigenous people of the Carribean) name for Corn; the Spaniards took that name to Mexico, where it was called *teozintli*; after the conquest, *maiz* became a more popular name.

Meoctli (Meh-ok-tlee): *Me* is maguey or agave; *octli* is nectar; agave nectar or honey.

Meyahuel (Meh-ya-wel): The Spirit Guardian of the Agave species of plants, especially the maguey; she represents the Moon's energy working to draw out Earth's nectars.

Mexikayotl (Me-she-kah-yotl): A Mesoamerican philosophy describing how all life is connected by "Moon's navel"; the word *Mexico* means "place where the Moon's navel touches Earth."

Micailhuitl (Mee-ka-eel-witl): Day of Death; one of the twenty days in the Aztec Calendar devoted to honoring the dead.

Mictlan (Mick-tlahn): Land where the Dead still live.

Mictlancihuatl (Mick-tlahn-see-watl): Death Woman; represents the female aspect of death.

Mictlantecutli (Mick-tlahn-the-kutlee): Death Chief; represents the male aspect of death.

Mikiztli (Mee-kiss-tlee): Death; the act of dying; the death journey.

Netzahualcoyotl (Net-sa-wal-ko-yotl): Hungry Coyote, the ruler around 1470 of the city of Texcoco, a city also constructed in the middle of a lake with the same name.

Oxomoco (Osho-mo-ko): The other half of the pair of the parents of the human race, the original couple.

Quetzalcoatl (Ket-sahl-co-ahtl): Feathered Serpent; precious twin and Morning Star; a deity that embodies the curving, snake-like motion of all natural forms; in humans, it represents an awakening, enlightenment; *Quetzalcoatl* is *Tezcatlipoca's* twin.

Tecpatl (tehk-pot-l): Obsidian Knife; one of the twenty days of the Aztec Calendar; also represents the years whose vibrations are directed toward the Northern Horizon.

Teocentli (te-osen-tlee): Spirit of the original Corn; when it was still only a grass and before it was transformed by a covenant with the People of Mexico.

Tepeyolotl (te-pe-yo-lotl): Heart of the mountain; an aspect of *Huitzilopochtli*; represents the inner strength that holds Earth forms together.

Teyolia (te-yo-li-ah): The Spirit that resides in the center of the heart; the electromagnetism that concentrated is in the pericardium.

Tezcatlipoca (tes-kah-tlee-poca): Smoking Mirror and Evening Star; a deity that embodies what is hidden or invisible in Nature; in humans, it is our dream time and the ability to remember and introspect; *Tezcatlipoca* is *Quetzalcoatl*'s twin.

Tlalcihuatl (tlal-see-watl): Earth Woman; a Mother Earth spirit.

Tlaloc (tlal-ok): Earth Nectar; a deity representing the exchange of water between Earth and Sky, what we know today as the water cycle; the *Tlalocs* are the weather makers.

Tlaltecutli (tlal-te-koo-tlee): Earth Chief; a male aspect of Mother Earth's spirit.

Tlazolteotl (tla-sol-te-ot-l): The Spirit Guardian of decaying matter with which she fertilizes the Earth; it is said she formed the rivers and lakes with her staff so the first People could access water.

Tochtli (toch-tlee): Rabbit; one of the twenty days of the Aztec Calendar; represents the years whose vibrations are directed toward the Southern Horizon.

Toltec (tol-tek): From the word *Toltecatl*, a follower of *Toltecayotl*; using your heart as an instrument to create beauty.

Tonalli (to-nahl-lee): Solar vibration; an electromagnetic sphere that appears atop a child's head while still in the womb and later descends into the body; a person's soul.

Tonal Machiotl (to-nal mahch-i-ot-l): Solar Knowledge; the wheel of the Aztec Calendar consisting of 365 days.

Tonalpohualli (to-nal-po-wal-lee): Solar Count; the wheel of the Aztec Calendar consisting of 260 days.

Tonalpohuak i(to-nal-po-wa-key): Title given to a person who has mastered the Aztec Calendar and can create divinatory charts for others.

Yolohuiztcalotl (yo-lo-witz-kah-lo-tl): Crow with a Hummingbird for a Heart; the author's Nahuatl name.

Xochimique (Sho-chee-mee-keh): Flowering Dead; a time set aside for the "flowering of the ancestors" when the spirits of the dead return to nurture the living.

About the Author

Carlos Aceves, born in 1954, has a Bachelor of Arts degree in journalism and a Master of Education in educational psychology. He is a bilingual teacher in Canutillo, Texas, and coordinates the Xinachtli Project for the Indigenous Cultures Institute. The Xinachtli Project utilizes Mesoamerican pedagogy to teach young children. He has presented at national conferences and various universities and institutions across the country. He began learning indigenous spirituality in 1980 from maestro Jesus Ventura and maestra Paola Juarez. Later, he traveled to Mexico, studying with several maestros of the Nahuatl and Mayan traditions. He has published in educational journals, chapters in texts for teacher education, and is author of the novel *Diadema* (Floricanto Press). *Yolohuitzcalotl* is his Nahuatl name, which means "Crow with a Hummingbird for a Heart."

www.ingramcontent.com/pod-product-compliance
Lightning Source LLC
Chambersburg PA
CBHW052207090426

42741CB00010B/2441